# Social Influence for Real Estate Sales Professionals: A Beginner's Guide

*By Gail Hansche*

**Case #:** 1-2169729491
**Title:** Social Influence For Real Estate Sales Professionals - A
Beginner's Guide

Library of Congress Cataloging-in-Publication Data
Hansche, Gail
Social Influence For Real Estate Sales Professionals -
Beginner's Guide

Editor: Maria Al Ameen
Jacket Design and Cover Art by Gail Hansche

ISBN-13:
978-1508655541

ISBN-10:
1508655545

# Dedication

This manual is gratefully dedicated to the hundreds of Real Estate Sales Professionals in the Philadelphia Metropolitan Region whom I've had the honor to meet and train. This manual was inspired by each of you.

Social media marketing is still in its infancy and continuously evolving. As a community of Real Estate Agents and Brokers, you noticed the profound lack of marketing strategies and best practices **specifically** for Real Estate Sales Practitioners. Understanding the process has been frustrating. Much like aiming at a moving target, without ammunition

In the field I saw your confusion and desire to understand this new-fangled mode of real estate marketing. Your questions were diligently noted and compiled over the course of 2 years. The answers to those questions resulted in the following pages intended to assist you and Agents and Brokers everywhere!

This manual is essentially a **"Facebook 101"** manual for Real Estate Sales Professionals and is intended for the **absolute beginner**. As such, topics have been deliberately dissected into tiny segments to enable you to move quickly across content, based on your personal learning needs

Like all things in life, take what you want from this manual and leave the rest behind. I welcome your questions, comments, feedback and suggestions for the next real estate dedicated social media manual in progress!

Here's to your success!

*Gail*

**Gail Hansche**
**ghansche@gmail.com**

# About the Author

 Originally licensed in 1987, Gail Hansche is an experienced Real Estate Salesperson, currently holding a New Jersey Broker's License. With over a quarter century of first hand listing and sales experience, management and mentor experience, Gail is currently a Real Estate Trainer in the Greater Philadelphia Metropolitan Region and an approved Continuing Education Instructor in the state of New Jersey.

# Acknowledgements

Gratitude to the family and friends that continually stand by me through the best and worst of times ---

Mom, Teresa, Stephen, Lia, Lyn and Paul; and to my son, the pride and joy of my life, Daniel.

# Table of Contents

# Facebook 101 for Real Estate Sales Professionals

This manual was created specifically for *Real Estate Sales Professionals* NEW to Facebook Marketing and/or perplexed by the process.

Here, you will learn how to:

- Neutralize your existing personal presence.
- Decide whether an aggressive Facebook marketing plan is for you.
- Create a real estate fan page.
- Employ best-practices, posting strategies and content curation.
- Implement an actionable "30-day Marketing Plan."
- Understand Facebook terminology.
- Access over 60 FREE resources and tools.

If you are like many, you've investigated social media plans for your real estate business in the past. You've probably noticed that most pre-packaged strategies don't quite work for real estate practitioners. In other words, the standard B2B and B2C social strategies aren't *"quite"* relevant to our unique industry. In fact, I use the term "Marketing" very loosely. As you'll see, in reality we are building a community of advocates without any of the typical marketing ploys.

Like anything in life, nothing here is written in stone. Use this manual as a guide post. Take what you want and leave the rest behind.

Let's begin...

You're already in business!

Did you know you're already working social media?

Think about it. If you are a real estate agent, broker, owner or sales manager with a personal Facebook presence, your services have already gone social; a reality that can haunt you or propel your business.

1

You work hard to cultivate your *sphere of influence* via email drips, mailers, farming, advertising, etc. with (hopefully) professional looking marketing pieces. Yet, you have the same or similar network of people that you real-time expose to potentially unprofessional, tacky and/or just overall inappropriate posts in real-time forum fashion on Facebook.

What image does your personal presence put forward? If you currently have a social business presence, what's the image perception there?

## If you do nothing else

Committing to a social marketing campaign is a lot like joining a gym. You can buy a membership, which in turn makes you a member, but if you don't use the membership by committing to a specific workout plan and showing up for it, you're really not working the program. Believe me, I know! More importantly, you won't get any results. The same is true for those of you that have or will decide to move forward with a formal social media community building plan.

Many of the agents I've worked with created a fan page and figure, *"OK, I'm on Facebook."* Creating a fan page and failing to do anything with it, can be more detrimental to your career than *not* having one at all.

Think of this as an abandoned piece of real estate that's been unattended for months, as the overgrown lawn obstructs the 'For Sale' sign on the front lawn. Certainly, an abandoned or neglected fan page is not the professional image we want to convey.

Like the gym membership analogy, social media marketing is a serious commitment. Be honest with yourself - realistically asses your interest, ability and available time.

Of course, there's always the option to outsource the job to an assistant or social media manager, if this is financially feasible for you. Or, you might simply decide to clean-up your personal presence for the sake of professional image preservation.

Social media is a relatively new way of marketing that is continually evolving. In addition to the time commitment required, ongoing changes can be understandably frustrating. The mechanics change-up often, making a click-by-click visual resource unrealistic. Lean on "Facebook Help" for any task you are struggling with. This is the most current and accurate source of functionality, in addition to being very easy to use.

Remember, you are not required to embrace every tool available to your real estate practice. If you did, you wouldn't be spending enough time in front of buyers and sellers making money. This is both the beauty and the curse of being an independent contractor, as you probably already know. It's your business, you make the final decisions.

Like most options in your real estate career, utilize tools you feel comfortable with, abandon the ones you don't care for and don't be afraid to re-examine all of your advertising and marketing choices regularly.

However, as this section title gives away, if you do nothing else, I urge you to utilize the first section of this manual to professionalize and neutralize your personal presence (if you have one). Image and credibility preservation is everything in our business.

## Relationships are everything!

Relationships are the key to success in the real estate business. Cultivating *relationships* is much like casting an enormous net into the depths of the ocean, capable of capturing numerous and constantly self-replicating leads throughout the course of your career. Year by year, if well-tended, your "catch" will multiply and expand.

For those of you in business for about 2 years, most likely you're beginning to see a decent amount of leads and referrals generating automatically. Those of you practicing for more than 20 years are starting to see generational sales. Meaning, you're now selling to the children of your original customers. An extremely rewarding process!

Have you noticed that *relationships* often trump any solid real estate expertise, acclaim or track record you may have? Here's a real life example of the power of relationships:

> My sister and her husband recently listed their home for sale in another state. Out of curiosity I asked if they'd used the agent

who'd sold them their home some 8+ years ago. After straining to recall the name of this long-ago agent, my sister responded, *"Oh no, we don't have any contact with her anymore."* OK, I thought silently. If the agent is still in business, bad job keeping in contact and leaving a lasting impression. Still curious, I asked *"How did you find the agent you are using?"* My sister replied, *"Oh, he's a fireman and his brother is a police officer who works with Tom* (her husband). *So, I guess technically he was recommended."* Attempting to process to connections while cringing internally, I'm wondering if this is the extent of the vetting performed on the person handling the single largest financial transaction of their lives. The power of relationships trumps all!

So, there you have it. Not a terribly unusual story. I'm sure you've all heard similar versions of the same.

Real estate sales success today has **less** to do with your track record, experience, success rate, brand, market share, etc. and everything to do with ***how likeable you are*** and ***how many relationships you've nurtured.*** Imagine the power of "likeability" coupled with "Experience." Now that's something to reach for!

**Retrospective -** when I began selling real estate in the mid 1980's, fax machines, cell phones and computers hadn't come around yet. It was also an extremely expensive time to be an agent. Marketing yourself and your listings meant coughing up large amounts of money to advertise in newspapers, full color home magazines and mailers. Back then, our MLS listings were delivered daily on 3-hole punched index cards via courier. Much of our time as agents was devoted to the culling, organizing and the overall maintenance of the information alone. Thank goodness that's all changed for the sake of time and accuracy. Although, I still hear a lot of preference for those long-ago simpler times from many veteran agents I meet in the field today.

**What we got wrong** – back then, was assuming our would-be customers actually cared about our carefully listed array of awards, fancy brochures and gleaming citations. We learned, the hard and expensive way, that in the end:

4

*"Customers really only care about themselves, what you can do for them, and how you make them feel in the process".*

This is an industry truism, both then and now.

In all fairness, back in those days of double digit interest rates, we agents had no other way to market ourselves. The internet hadn't happened yet. Of course, today there are additional expenses related to online marketing, software and tools that do seem to balance out the past and present.

But here's the thing... Today, you can do much, if not all, of your marketing yourself with a free Facebook account and an internet connection. You don't need a bank roll to create a presence in order to nurture those important **relationships**. What you will need is a plan, a commitment of time and perseverance.

## Social benefits

Getting your name out there has never been easier, and it's free! Social media gives agents the ability to take advantage of:

- <u>Level playing field</u> - access to the same forum as large businesses and brands.
- <u>Direct communication</u> – with past, present and future customers in a real time, informal and laid-back environment.
- <u>Relationship building environment</u> – where trust, credibility and top-of-mind awareness through engagement can be incubated.

**How real estate differs from "big brand" marketing** - consider visiting the Pepsi brand fan page. You'll see Pepsi at Christmas, Pepsi at the Super Bowl, Pepsi at the beach, coupons, contests, discounts and why you should buy and drink Pepsi.

Since Pepsi is a tangible and consumable product, this works well. Imagine, however, applying what you see on Pepsi's page to your real estate practice - probably not a very good idea. This is not to say that there aren't some awesome ideas and inspirations to be found and tweaked from major brand pages, because there are.

Take a look at the pages of your local CPA, dentist, congressman or any other local professional you know. Size up their posts and content. This *"local professional"* approach to social marketing is closer to what we real estate agents are shooting for.

Who is your customer?

Evaluate:
- the *who*,
- the *what,* and
- the *where*, of your clientele.

Take a look at your sales over the past 2 years. What types of sales did you close and to whom? If you are new, use whatever sales you have thus far. If you are new and have none, ask your office manager/broker for office or company level norms as a starting point. Most agents will find they work primarily with 1 or 2 well-defined niches.

The point here is in the examination of your typical client. For example, if you happen to work a niche market comprised of primarily active adult communities, consisting of exclusively "veteran generation" home buyers and sellers (people born between 1925 and 1945), social media may not give you much traction.

**Audience Appeal** - Once you've defined your primary audiences (niches), ask yourself, what form of communication and promotion works best for them? This could range from social media, email blasts, snail mail campaigns or sponsoring charitable events.

For example, the National Association of REALTORS® (NAR's) definition of today's early 30-something first time homebuyer, also known as the "millennial" generational identity (born after 1980), will almost always use the web and social media for information and purchases. They'll also have significantly different content interests and communication preferences when compared to their "baby boomer" parents.

Here's an example. My 79 year old mother doesn't own a computer, still writes out checks to pay her bills and communicates with hand written snail mail notes to everyone. To reach her, you'd be best to call, drop-by with a

6

Bundt cake, or send some kind of offer in the mail that might catch her eye. You certainly won't find her on the internet or social media. You will, however, find her looking through a physical copy of the newspaper and consulting her phone book to locate the services she needs.

Eclipse the above with my 20-something year old son who recently transacted his late father's estate, entirely by text, email and electronic signature. Vastly different modus operandi!

Simply put, is your *sphere of influence* or target market sufficiently involved in social networking to make it worth your effort?

## Which social platform?

We all know there are numerous social media options. Of course, you're not limited to one single platform. However, consider the following. By the sheer mechanics of the platform, Facebook is truly the ideal environment to nurture existing **relationships** and cultivate new ones. Think about it -

> *Your entire sphere of influence is already on Facebook, in addition to virtually every past, present and future client you'll ever have!*

That's a darn good reason! The power of Facebook is truly astounding!

**So, why Facebook? -** The short answer is as above, because **everyone is there**! Let's take it a step further and dig-in to a bit of *Facebook psychology*.

Why do you think so many people join Facebook? To share their personal stories and lives, to check-in on the lives of their friends and family, and consciously or subconsciously determine how they "stack-up" to their peers. More importantly, I think it is safe to say that no one has ever joined Facebook with the intention of buying something or being sold something. This is important!

Think about the way products and services are found and utilized today. TV ads, mailers, even the once popular mass-email blast marketing of the late 90's/early 00's are increasingly ineffective and archaic. The bulk of today's buyers and sellers simply go online to research information and rely on peer recommendations for connections. This shift is becoming increasingly ubiquitous as the aforementioned "millennial" generation grows up and moves towards homeownership.

Acknowledging and adjusting your processes demonstrates your ability to adapt to the evolving needs of your clients and your ability to remain vital to our industry for the long haul.

Yes, there are many social media platforms to choose from and I encourage you to investigate and use as many as you like. There are huge advantages to tying multiple platforms together once you get going. There are also some terrific products available that will help you manage them. However, *"the buck really does start on Facebook."*

## The statistics

Get rid of your notion that Facebook is just for kids, or a time waster. Here are some compelling facts and statistics from Pew Research (2013), CNBC, 2012 State of Inbound Marketing and the National Association of REALTORS® (NAR):

- Approximately 77% of B2C (business to consumer) organizations generated a customer with Facebook.

- 57% of American adults use Facebook.

- Adult Facebook use is intensifying: 64% of Facebook users visit the site on a daily basis.

- Half of all adult Facebook users have more than 200 friends in their network.

- Facebook has more monthly users (1.32 billion) than India's population, the world's second-most populous country (1.24 billion).

- There are more than one trillion posts on Facebook.

- At 1.35 billion, Facebook has more monthly active users than Twitter (255 million) and Instagram (200 million).

- More than 1 billion people use Facebook on a mobile device monthly. That's about 1/7th of the population of planet earth.

- 44% of Facebook users like content posted by their friends at least once a day, with 29% doing so several times per day.

- 31% comment on other people's photos on a daily basis, with 15% doing so several times per day.

- 19% send private Facebook messages to their friends on a daily basis, with 10% sending these messages multiple times per day.

- 10% change or update their own status on Facebook on a daily basis, with 4% updating their status several times per day.

**Reasons for Facebook Use - Men vs. Women (Source: 2013 Pew Research)** - Did you know …?

*Women* are more likely than *men* to cite the following major reasons for using Facebook:

- Viewing photos and videos.
- Sharing with many people at once.
- Seeing entertaining or funny posts.
- Learning about ways to help others.
- Receiving support from their network of friends.

Conversely, *Men* are more likely than **Women** to cite the following major reasons for Facebook use:

- Seeing photos or videos.
- Ability to share with many people at once.
- Receiving updates or comments.
- Keeping up with news and current events.

**Who has friends?** - Take a look at the median number of Facebook friends by age bracket. Truly astounding:

| | Age | # of Friends |
|---|---|---|
| • | 18-29 | 300 |
| • | 30-49 | 200 |
| • | 50-64 | 75 |
| • | 65+ | 30 |

**We really don't like that!** - For all the liking that occurs on Facebook, there's quite a lot people don't like.  For example, users strongly dislike:

- People sharing too much information (TMI) about themselves – 36%
- Others posting things or photos of them, without permission – 36%
- Others seeing posts or photos you didn't want them to see – 27%
- Pressure to post content and comments that will be popular and get lots of likes – 12%
- Pressure to comment on content posted by others in their network – 12%
- Seeing posts about social activities you were not included in – 5%

Today's buyers and sellers

Who are today's buyers and sellers? According to the 2013 National Association of REALTORS® Profile of Home Buyers and Sellers:

Sellers:

- The typical home seller in 2013 was 53 years of age, had a median household income of $97,500 and lived in their home for 9 years.

- 88% of sellers were assisted by a real estate agent when selling their home.

- Recent sellers typically sold their homes for 97% of the listing price, and 47% reported reducing the asking price at least once.

- The typical home sold was on the market for 5 weeks.

- 39% of sellers who used a real estate agent found their agents through a referral by friends or family and 25% used the agent they previously worked with to buy or sell a home.

- Sellers who definitely would use same agent again - 65%

Buyers:

- First-time buyers -38%

- Median age of first-time buyers -31

- Median age of repeat buyers – 52

- Median household income of first-time buyers - $64,400

- Median household income of repeat buyers - $96,000

- The typical home purchased in 2013 was 1,900 square feet in size, built in 1992, and had three bedrooms and two bathrooms.

- Among those who financed their home purchase, buyers typically financed 90% of the home price.

- 88% of buyers purchased their home through a real estate agent or broker—a share that has steadily increased from 69% in 2001.

- Buyers who definitely would use same agent again -73%

- Information sources used in home search:
  - Real estate agent: 89%
  - Yard sign: 51%

- Use of mobile of tablet website or application - 45%

- Open house - 45%

- Print newspaper advertisement - 23%

## Your social strategy, in a nutshell

Essentially, you're soft-dripping on your entire *sphere of influence*, comprising past customers, future customers, friends, friends of friends and even family. Perfect! With this in mind, your goals in a nutshell are:

- **Create** a community of advocates.
- **Engage** in an ongoing "living dialogue" with your sphere of influence.
- **Build** and cultivate relationships.
- **Expand** your sphere of influence by converting friends of friends.
- **Maintain** top of mind awareness (no hard sell, don't peddle your wares).
- **Generate** leads and referrals.

**Make sure online and offline interactions closely mirror one another** - There's a tendency towards a more hard-sell sales approach online since you are not face to face with your potential customer. Don't do that! Instead, consider this:

> **The Cocktail Party Analogy** - If you were invited to a cocktail party, you probably wouldn't walk around the venue performing *"who's buying or selling"* interrogatories on everyone you encountered, nor would you be *"elevator pitching"* guests with your latest listings and sales. If you did, I think it's safe to assume there'd be no future social invitations from that social circle.

Similarly, if you behaved badly at the event - say you had a bit too much to drink, got loud, flirty or disrespectful, even mildly - this too might reek permanent damage to your social reputation, as well as your real estate career.

The cocktail party analogy sums up your social role as the local real estate professional quite accurately. First, no hard selling. Secondly, there's really very little separation between your personal and business lives or your online and offline image.

Here's the good news. If NAR built a social platform specifically for real estate agents and their clients, I doubt it would look much different from today's Facebook environment. It's really a near perfect tool based on how we build our businesses. We can't change some of the inherent pitfalls of the platform, but we can create opportunity from deficiencies and work them to our advantage. That said,

*The blending of positive personal and professional images is your "SECRET SAUCE!"*

Perception, your primary social brand

Here's what we know. In this digital world we are often judged and interviewed without ever knowing it. Prospective clients and friends have the opportunity to form a perception of us, sight unseen, based exclusively on what they hear from friends, family and past customers, both online and offline.

Much can be revealed about you personally by a quick web search. We're not just talking about social media; we're talking about what is referred to as your entire **digital footprint** *(the trail, traces or "footprints" that people leave online.)*

If you currently have a personal or real estate fan page, what perception do these convey? Will your personal profile reveal a succession of *high game scores*, *TMI* and *politically incorrect posts and photos*? Will fan page visitors see a meager 23 likes, a post from six months ago and an empty profile?

**Gamers use caution!** - I had a real estate colleague in the 80's that did a lot of business in her immediate community. Every morning, she made certain her car was in the garage by 9am, so neighborhood clients wouldn't know she was home, instead of working diligently to sell their homes. Today that dynamic has shifted a bit.

If it's 2pm on a Saturday afternoon and one of your seller clients sees one of those *"cow requests"* come across their newsfeed from you, might this cause a perception problem?

**Maintain neutrality** - It is crucial that you keep your posts neutral, apolitical and secular. Here's another real life example:

During the 2008 presidential election, a very seasoned and successful agent I worked with went on a Facebook political rant. It doesn't matter what side of the aisle she was on, but within a week, she'd limited her future sales exclusively to those on the side of the fence she so fervently endorsed. That hard-earned career tanked in lightning speed.

Another agent I met in the field, not too long ago, 'friended' me. I immediately began seeing extremely intense religious warnings and biblical verses applied to the woes of current events.

Don't get me wrong, I admire people who are passionate about their beliefs. I'm sure you are too. But there's a place for it. When you are in business, you don't have the luxury of offending the personal beliefs of your customers without going out of business.

Returning to the *cocktail party analogy*, how would it go over if you started spouting your fervent beliefs at a live event? Probably not so well, yet it happens all the time on Facebook.

Basic rule of thumb - post nothing that you wouldn't announce in public or adhere to a billboard on the largest roadway or highway in your state.

Got expertise?

We've discussed how buyers and sellers typically choose someone they like and feel comfortable with, over someone who may, in reality, be better skilled and experienced to get the job of selling one's home accomplished.

While an un-pleasant reality, this does not mean you are *off the hook* when it comes to learning and mastering everything there is to know about how real estate is transacted in the areas you sell. I'm often taken aback by the lack of basic real estate knowledge many agents have to offer.

Ask yourself … why should a buyer or seller hire me? As real estate professionals, we handle what is for most, their largest financial asset. Shouldn't we know what we're talking about … even a little?

While it is exciting to embark on a new social media endeavor to build our business, our first and foremost obligation is always to our clients. One of the cornerstones of this obligation is always expertise!

Marketing, of any kind, is simply marketing. You may gain short term leads as a result, but true longevity hinges on your knowledge and expertise. Learn your business first. After all, you are paid for your advice, guidance and ability to navigate the home buying and selling processes. Take advantage of the years of experience and knowledge surrounding you in your office and local real estate associations.

**Keeping real estate professionals relevant to the process** - Today's real estate consumer has mastered the housing search. We are no longer the *"gate keepers"* of information, but we are the *"translators."* Stay informed and keep ahead of the curve. Make sure you understand the buying and selling processes top to bottom to retain your relevance to the home buying and selling processes. Your expertise will keep you top of mind, long after the transaction settles.

**Size-up your real estate knowledge!** - Some agents service a broader territory or geographic area than others. The broader your service area, the more knowledge you'll need to know to properly assist your clients.

**Do consumers need real estate professionals?** - YESSS! There's a lot of discussion in the industry about the diminished role of the real estate professional. Agents tell me *"why do they need us, they can get everything they need online."* Well, I'd agree if your professional role was summed up by the distribution of real estate data and opening lockboxes.

Consider this:

> Today, laypersons can obtain a plethora of information on medical procedures, medications, diseases and treatments. Does this on-demand information mean we don't consult a doctor? Of course not! We go to get guidance, weigh options, get their professional

opinion and an explanation of the information we've found. Hopefully, we are then given a course of treatment specific to our situation.

The above holds true for real estate sales professionals, assuming you have the knowledge to assess and solve the problems of the consumers that use your services.

**Your value to consumers** - Real estate agents have the potential to provide tremendous value through:

- Area knowledge.
- Ability to assess and plainly explain options.
- Expert navigation of the home buying and selling processes.

**Expertise -- your BEST social fuel** - Your expert real estate knowledge will give you some significant social fuel when you offer content specific to local real estate related issues in your market(s). Minimize the social promotion of listings and open houses. Preferably, swap them out in favor of your advice and articles of interest, specific to the issues important to your sphere of influence. Showcase your expertise by giving content of real value to your audience, as a result of your knowledge. Here are some ideas:

- Area schools, districts, boundaries, value impacts and reports. Many local MLS's and local real estate associations offer incredible tools like RPR and FIND, which dig deeply into community profiles, best school ratings and much more.
- Problem areas and solutions– high water tables, flooding, radon, mold, construction issues.
- Sub-divisions/communities – Who built them, when, model details, square footage, price range, community amenities?
- Municipal certifications – How strict is each municipality on fire certifications, building/addition permits, continued occupancy certifications and how do they all hinge on one another area by area?
- Programs – what are the sports, arts and music offerings in each school and/or district?

- What are the nuances in the different areas you sell? For example, if you work in a large condominium complex of re-sales, does the development regularly qualify for Fannie and Freddie approval?
- What municipal or lender certifications are required in the areas you serve?
- How do you handle issues that arise like radon, mold, well, septic and wood destroying insects?

**What NOT to do!** - If you currently have any existing Facebook presence, do any of the following activities describe your current marketing approach?

- A focus on getting likes for your personal or fan page?
- Inclusion of **other agents** on your fan page?
- Treating your fan or personal page like a *"branding brochure"* or *"bulletin board"* for every new listing, price reduction and open house you have?
- Constantly seeking the ultimate *"silver bullet"* that solicits immediate business?

## ZMOT!

We've established that buyers and sellers actively use search engines and social networks to locate people to do business with.

Due to the overabundance of on-demand information on the web, agents now enter the buying and selling process later, at a moment of enormous opportunity. This moment is called the zero moment of truth (ZMOT).

Basically, ZMOT is the point of action and decision. For example, most people become aware of a need or desire to buy a new car, but don't act on it immediately. There's a lot internal processing that goes on between first awareness and driving home in a new car. The salesperson who is "top of mind" when the decision is made, wins!

If you are a traditional real estate agent, expecting your *sphere of influence* or past clientele to call you when they're ready to buy or sell based on your quarterly newsletter mailings and/or annual holiday card, you might be disappointed. The agent that's top of mind when ZMOT occurs wins the race! Facebook marketing provides you with this opportunity - the ability to be on hand at ZMOT!

A new sales culture

While hard sell tactics in other industries live on, it is a thing of the past in real estate sales (thankfully). Although it seems counterintuitive, you actually sell more when you stop selling. Here's what today's' buyers and sellers expect:

- Authenticity, not spin.
- Participation, not propaganda.
- Options, not sales pitch.
- Plain language, not industry jargon.
- Advocacy, not a salesperson.

**Keep it simple -** You don't need to be tech savvy or learn all kinds of new skills. Think of your social media presence as an extension of your day-to-day dealings with your customers. Just be yourself! Chances are the traits that make you successful face-to-face, are the same traits that will enhance your online relationships.

Start slow. You'll know intuitively when to ramp up and take your marketing efforts to the next level. For the single or team real estate practitioners, the number of welcome pages, opt-in forms, videos, blogs and apps you've added to your fan page are completely irrelevant.

If you currently have, or decide to create a fan page, you'll have the ability to analyze performance with Facebook's free "Page Insight" tool. Insights will become your compass for future decisions.

As your presence matures, simply adapt and refine social media marketing strategies as needed, while keeping up with relevant trends.

What's next?

From here, we'll take a look at:

- Your existing *Personal Page/Profile* (FP) – Part I
- Creation of a *Fan Page/Like Page* (FFP) - Part II

•

# PART I: Protecting your Online Reputation and Neutralizing your Personal Page and Profile (FP)

First, let's be clear on the terminology often used interchangeably and sometimes erroneously:

- **Personal Profiles** aka **Personal Pages (FPs)** have **Friends**
- **Fan Pages** aka **Business Pages** aka **Like Pages (FFPs)** have **Fans**
- You can have but **ONE** *Personal Profile (FP)*
- Yet, **MULTIPLE** *Fan Pages (FFPs)*

Yes, the above can be to absorb, but necessary nonetheless.

## "Melting pot" benefits

Real estate agents do business with friends, family, friends of friends, acquaintances and total strangers that we cumulatively call our *sphere of influence*.

This is precisely why Facebook's "*melting pot*" environment is the perfect incubation mechanism for cultivating real estate **relationships** and future clients. Your existing list of friends is likely a mass merge of all your connections. In reality, more extensive than your day-to-day offline connections. A huge benefit!

Attending to numerous connections within one forum may seem overwhelming, but once your systems and processes are in place, you'll enjoy the interactions and ever-deepening **relationships**.

**A lead generation "*slow cooker*"** - If you are looking to produce immediate, saleable leads, Facebook marketing is not the platform for you. Facebook is a *credibility slow cooker,* for real estate professionals interested in investing in past, present and future **relationships** as a means to sustain their business for years to come.

## Getting started

If you don't have an account, I recommend starting out by working a FP until you get the feel of things. Build your network of friends and launch your FFP (if you choose), once you've got a decent personal network of friends and feel comfortable with the platform.

If you are the owner or a responsible member of a real estate office or organization, it likely makes the most sense to start a business page with your corporate email address under the "company/organization" or "brand/product" page categories. You can assign page administration roles to trusted colleagues for regular content contribution to diversify discussions and topics.

## Protect your reputation

Know what's been published on the web about you and your company. Run an internet search on your name and company name. Attend to anything unfavorable as needed.

Going forward, set-up a few Google alerts at www.google.com/alert to keep yourself informed. Google alerts will monitor the web for you, based on specific topics or keywords you want to follow.

For now, create separate alerts for your full name(s) including any aliases (ex. maiden name) and your company. Then set it and forget about it.

Google alerts are also a great tool for fresh content curation.

## Cover and thumbnail photos

Cover and thumbnail photos are public, regardless of your other FP privacy settings.

You may be a passionate hunter, or a staunch supporter of the legalization of cannabis. Regardless, your cover photo probably shouldn't be that of a cannabis leaf and your thumbnail photo probably shouldn't show you holding up your latest hunting trophy by its hind legs. Things like this are never good for business.

Keep your personal interests in lists and groups where you can collaborate with like-minded friends that share your passion.

## Find new friend connections

There are a few different ways to build your friends list. Click on the friend icon in the upper right hand corner of your FP to access the following options:

- <u>People you may know</u> - these are suggestions from Facebook based on your profile information and current network of friends. Send invitations to those you'd like to connect with. You will begin receiving friend requests yourself, which you can accept or ignore.
- <u>Find friends -</u> enter the individual email addresses of people you know personally and invite them to accept your friendship invitation.
- <u>Import email addresses</u> - import email addresses from virtually any account (Outlook, Yahoo, Hotmail, Gmail, etc.) and send invites to the friends you choose.

**Contact file** - Create a quick 1-column list of your contacts' email addresses (only). Upload them for registered user matches.

## What are lists?

Lists are a way to organize things on Facebook, like your friends or the things you're interested in. You can use lists to filter the stories you see in your newsfeed, or post an update for specific people such as co-workers or past clients.

For example, if you created a list inclusive of all *"Shady Oak Condo Homeowners,"* you'd be able to send specific community updates exclusively to the people you added to this list.  This drives privacy and keeps content relevant to the people that care about similar things.

Lists are easy to create. Detailed instructions can be found in Facebook Help.

## Evaluate new and existing friends

Jot down all your *existing* Facebook friends to a 5-column chart (nothing fancy, handwritten is fine). Denote the following information for each friend:

- <u>Name</u>
- <u>How you met</u> - college, family, club, PTA, previous employment, fellow real estate agent, past customer, current customer, etc.
- <u>Interests</u> - Write at least one known interest for each friend (i.e. gardening, photography, crafts, lives in Cherry Hill, cooking, insurance broker, hockey fan, etc.)
- <u>Housing status</u> – Rent, own or with parents? How did they purchase their current home, if applicable?
- <u>List/group </u>– Decide which list(s) and/or group(s) each friend should be added to.

On a separate sheet of paper, keep a running list of the custom groups and lists you'll need to create, along with the names of those to be added to each. Friends can be added to multiple lists and groups. You are not limited to one per friend.

When you complete this task, you'll get a strong visual of your connections and how they are inter-connected. You'll definitely gain some insights you hadn't thought of before.

Example:

| <u>Name</u> | <u>Met</u> | <u>Interests</u> | <u>Housing Status</u> | <u>List/Groups</u> |
|------|-----|-----------|----------------|-------------|
| Lyn | RE School | Karaoke<br>Grandkids | Owns (licensed) | Restricted<br>RE Group |
| Teri | Sister | Animals<br>Gambling | Owns-upgrade<br>soon | Family<br>Past Client<br>List |
| Rose | College | Yoga<br>Meditation<br>Dogs | Owns-selling soon<br>Past Client | Close friend<br>Past Client<br>Yoga group<br>College<br>Friends |

| Jorge | Referral | Little League | Renting-will buy | Past Client |
|-------|----------|---------------|------------------|-------------|
|       |          | Cuban Pride   | Possible Relocation | Acquaint. |
|       |          | Cooking       |                  | 1st time    |

## Create custom lists

Based on your analysis, EVERY existing friend needs to be assigned to a relevant list. Facebook gives you default list categories to populate for *friends, family, acquaintances and restricted.* Use these if they work. More importantly, add as many of your own custom lists as needed.

Note the mix of personal and business here. As above, friends can be added to multiple lists and groups. For example, if your past client is also in your yoga class, add them to your past client and yoga class group.

Here are some list ideas to get you started:

- College friends
- PTA friends
- Yoga friends
- Past clients
- Sphere of influence
- Prospects
- 1st time homebuyers
- Shady Oaks condo owners
- Glen Ridge Golf Club members

## Smart lists

In addition to the custom lists you create and the default list categories provided by Facebook, you might notice some smart lists. Smart lists create themselves and automatically update based on the profile information you and your friends have in common (ex: work, school, family, city).

For example, if you entered Cornell as the university you attended and your friends Dan and Kate listed this too, you might see a smart list called

"Cornell University" with Dan and Kate in it. Smart lists are basically suggestions from Facebook. You are not required to use them.

## Restrict liberally!

Every friend that is **not** in your inner circle of trusted family and intimate friends, should be assigned to your FP's restricted list. I know what you're thinking. This seems harsh, but you really need to trust me on this. You can always change things up later on.

Adding friends to your restricted list maintains your FP friend connection, but your posts are only visible to this list when you select public audience distribution, or when you tag them personally in a post. Don't worry about hurting feelings, they won't know unless they happen to compare the visual content they see with that of an unrestricted mutual friend. Highly unlikely.

## Groups

Once your lists are set-up, create custom groups surrounding your personal interests, affiliations, political preferences and/or causes. A group is best defined as a community or forum. Groups should consist of users that share your interest(s) and with whom you wish to collaborate.

Create custom groups - Click the **Groups** header on the left-hand navigation panel of your personal newsfeed to create a new group. Name the group and start inviting your friends. It's that simple!

Groups should be related to topics that would NOT be of general interest to your network of friends in its entirety. For example, religious, political, work and special interests.

Remember the earlier examples of the agents that went on political and religious social meltdowns? Groups would have been the perfect solution for them, as they enable collaboration with like-minded individuals in a non-public, private forum.

Lists are a way to organize your friends and things you're interested in. Lists are available only on FPs, for the purpose of audience selection and filtering. Only you can see and access your lists.

Conversely, a group is a shared forum accessible and visible to all group members where documents and photos can be shared and collaborated on.

For example, if you created an *"Anytown Realty Group"* and added every agent in your office to the group, each group member would have access to the forum. You'd be able to share new listing information, open house invitations, motivated seller notices, price reductions, etc. Groups are the perfect way for agents to communicate about topics others won't care about.

- Group Types: You can create *public, private, or secret* groups
- Privacy: There are more privacy settings available for groups. In secret and closed groups, posts are only visible to group members.
- Audience: You can adjust group privacy to require members to be approved or added by those with group administrative roles. When a group reaches a certain size, some features are limited. The most useful groups tend to be the ones you create with small groups of people you know.
- Communication: In groups, members receive notifications by default when any member posts in the group (individual members can adjust this setting). Group members can participate in chats, upload photos to shared albums, collaborate on group documents and create events.

Going forward, use a combination of groups and lists on your FP to communicate with specific audiences each time you post. Simply choose the appropriate list or group each time you post!

## Other agents

Whether an agent is in your physical office, or is someone you know and work with regularly, all other real estate professionals are <u>competitors</u> and should be added to specific custom groups and lists. Again, I know this seems harsh. The reality is everyone with a real estate license in your service area is a competitor!

**Against terms of service** - Important! Most agents don't realize that it's against Facebook's terms of service to promote listings, open houses, etc. on your FP. Refrain from promotional business posts to your FP!

## Be vigilant

As a business person in a social environment:

- Keep your personal stuff personal.
- Keep your religious and/or political beliefs in private group forums or lists.
- Keep your non-professional photos private.
- Keep your humor and visuals light and G rated.

## Avoid social meltdowns

Perhaps you recall Congressman Andrew Weiner's ordeal and the resulting *"weinergate"* scandal?  Of course I'm not suggesting you'd stoop to such antics, but not every social meltdown is of a national epic proportion either. A seemingly minor and innocent moment of poor judgment could reap equally devastating consequences to your real estate career and personal life.

In other words, if you want to share your family vacation pictures with a private group or specific list of close friends and family, this is appropriate. Public shares are always risky.

## Take a realistic look

Perhaps photos of your family vacation, or your victorious, yet potentially infamous win at the craps table with beer in hand, need to be attended to. Remember, everyone on your FP is a potential buyer or seller. Your "*Activity Log*" is a tool that allows you to review and manage your past posts and activities.

## Scrub it down!

Visit your *activity log* to:

- Review your previous posts, photos and stories.
- Use the *audience selector tool* (denoted with each entry) to see the audience the post was shared with. Adjust as necessary.
- Delete or hide posts from your timeline, as needed.

Keep in mind that the posts you hide or delete from your timeline may still be visible to the audience originally shared with, depending on individual user settings and subsequent shares.

## Tagging

When you tag someone, you create a link to their profile. The post you tag the person in may also be added to that person's timeline. For example, you can tag a photo to show who's in the photo, or post a status update and say who you're with.

**Tag review on!** - Even the most well intentioned family or friend may innocently tag you in a potentially career compromising photo. *Tag review* requires your approval before posts are released to your timeline. Tags will accumulate in your *activity log*, pending your approval or deletion. An extremely wise precautionary measure.

> A friend of mine, in a very high visibility professional position, was aghast by a childhood friends' public share of a 40 year old 4th grade geeky class photo. Had tag review been engaged, embarrassment would have been avoided.

## Post moderation

The point of Facebook is to encourage engagement and interaction. However, you know first-hand if you've got a problematic friend, ex or unhappy customer that might post something derogatory to your FP. If you think this is a possibility, manage who can post to your timeline in your privacy settings.

## Blocking

If you need to take things a step further, *blocking* is always an option. Do not hesitate to use it. Your reputation (and your sanity) are at stake.

## Going forward

Now that your page infrastructure is in place, your primary goal is relatively simple:

- Prior to every future post, consider *who/what the appropriate audience(s) are.*
- Post *public* ONLY with extreme care and caution.
- Keep your lists current and create new lists and groups as often as necessary.
- Reassign new and existing friends as needed.

## Can't I just use my personal page and profile?

Absolutely! Upon completing the above, you've performed this manual's most critical recommendation. You've "cleaned-up" your personal presence. This is sufficient for infrequent users and those uninterested in more aggressively working a fan page for targeted engagement.

To do this, simply create and utilize lists and groups in order to define appropriate audiences for future posts.

Should you wish to take things to the next level, move on to Part II.

# PART II: Creating a Real Estate Fan Page (FFP)

Welcome Back! As we touched on earlier, creating an FFP is recommended, but not required.

Consider your ability to devote about ½ hour per day, once the initial set-up of your FFP is complete. If this is unrealistic, think twice before taking the plunge. If you decide to forge ahead, you'll have some choices to make. The following will assist you with this.

## Fan page options

Facebook is big on transparency to avoid spamming. They frown on users creating multiple FPs or using aliases to do so. They also like to see FFPs connected to FPs.  Additionally, you'll be required to use your full name for your FP, not some "anonymous handle." Some options to consider:

- <u>Convert</u> - your existing personal Facebook page (FP) to a fan page (FFP). Drawback: Lose your personal page – <u>not recommended</u>!
- <u>Keep, add and connect</u> – keep your FP and create a 2nd fan page (FFP) that is connected to your FP. This allows you to easily invite existing FP friends to your new FFP and customize crossover content and commenting.
- <u>Start from scratch</u> - create a business page from scratch with your corporate email address. You will be unable to automatically invite friends from your FP. However, administrative roles can be assigned to bridge this gap. This option is recommended for office of company pages.

## Fan Page vs. Business Page

These terms are often used interchangeably, despite the fact that there really is a difference based on the page category selected at set-up. Current page categories are:

- Local business
- Place
- Company, organization or institution
- Brand or product
- Artist, band, public figure, entertainment
- Cause or community

Individual real estate practitioners fall under the *local business* category. Conversely, offices and organizations may not.

**Personal presence vs. fan page -** FPs are for non-commercial use and represent individual people. You can follow profiles to see public updates from people you're interested in. FFPs look similar to FPs, but they offer unique tools for businesses, brands and organizations:

- FPs utilize friends, lists and groups.
- FFPs have fans only.
- FFP posts are public and are generally available to everyone on Facebook.
- FFP likes are open to all. FPs are subject to friend approval.
- There is no limit to number of people that can like a FFP.
- Friends on FPs cap at 5,000.
- FFPs can create customized apps for their page.
- FFPs have access to Page Insights to track audience reach and performance.

Page conversion

If you decide to convert your FP to an FFP, the information from your current profile, picture, and all current friends will be transferred and converted to fans. Your account's username will become the username for your page, and the name associated with your FP will become your new FFP's name.

If you want your FFP to have a different name, conversion won't work. Content will not be carried over to your new page. In this case, be sure to save any important information before conversion. There is a download option available for this.

You'll be unable to manage any groups from your FP and will need to appoint new group administrators prior to conversion.

## Creating a new fan page

Creating a FFP that is connected to your FP (recommended option) has a number of perks. You'll have the ability to invite your existing FP friends to your new FFP and cross post from one page to another.

To create your page, click "create page" from the left hand navigation panel on your FP. Alternatively, use the "create a page" from any existing page.

## What's in a name?

Everyone names their FFP something like *"Rob Smith, Real Estate Agent."* Get creative and specific with page names to harness the power of keyword searches both on and off Facebook. Which of the below do you think is a more powerful and compelling option?

- "John Doe, Realtor"
- "John Doe, Philadelphia's Condo Expert"
- "Top 100 Places in Philadelphia" --this would be considered a community page (see more below).

## Community pages

Community pages are dedicated to a topic or experience that is owned collectively by the community connected to it. Similar to pages for businesses, organizations and public figures, Community pages let you connect with others who share similar interests and experiences. I've seen tremendous agent success in the community page niche.

A community page is a brilliant and under-utilized agent marketing strategy. The creation of separate (potentially multiple) community pages around area community interests and local topics within an agent's primary service area make powerful lead funnels. Here are some suggestions to get you thinking:

- *"Shady Oaks Homeowners Community"*
- *"Things We Love About Burlington County NJ"*
- *"Top 100 Things to Do in Philadelphia"*
- *"Scottsdale AZ County Housing Stats"*

## SEO your page

To help your page be found on Facebook and in search engines, stock your FFP profile and "*about* section" with your location, and areas served with as many relevant keywords as possible.

SEO keyword examples: *Condo, Real Estate, Philadelphia, First Time Homebuyers, Investment Properties, Vacation Properties, Luxury Properties, For Sale, Active Adult Communities, and so on.*

You can go deeper with this topic by utilizing Google AdWords to define popular keywords, however, there is a fee. Check-out free alternatives by typing "keywords" into your search engine and experiment.

## Cover & thumbnail photos

Get creative, yet professional with your cover photo. Consider a DIY custom cover using canva.com, or visit fiverr.com and have one professionally created for about $5.

Keep your thumbnail photo professional and high quality. I've seen way too many blurry and cropped personal photos here. There are inexpensive professional photography options available in most every locality. Ask for real estate agent head shot specials. I've gotten these for as low as $20. Consider a standing or action photo (ex. greeting clients, installing a sold sign, etc.).

## Settings

You'll need to make selections regarding page moderation, messages, posting ability and your FFPs profanity filter. Please review this section thoroughly. I recommend you moderate your page by activating the control available to monitor posts by others. This will give you the opportunity to approve any posts before they publish to your page's wall.

Before the official unveiling of your new FFP:

- Spend at least a week prior to the official launch via fan invitation, to stock your store with compelling content. An empty storefront is never a good thing! See content curation ideas below for ideas.

## Build your audience

Your primary audience building options are as follows:

- <u>Invite relevant friends from your FP</u> - to invite your FP friends to your FFP, use <u>Facebook as yourself</u> and not as your FFP. Access "build audience."
- <u>Reach out to your trusted advocates</u> - ask your core group of business advocates to suggest your FFP on their page.
- <u>By invitation</u> - invitations can be sent to any user with an account registered to the email addresses you upload.

## Import email addresses

As you did for your FP, import your contact files from numerous sources including Gmail, Yahoo, and Hotmail to generate invitations to your new FFP.

Many email clients and PIM programs allow contacts to be exported to a file. The following types of contact files are supported:

- comma-separated values (.csv)
- vCards (.vcf)
- tab-delimited text (.txt)
- LDAP

TIP: this was mentioned in Part I and is worthy of repeating. If you are like many, your contact information is here, there and everywhere. If so, create a simple 1-column Excel spreadsheet containing your contacts' email addresses (only). Simply save the file in a .csv format instead of an Excel workbook format and upload to Facebook.

Don't be afraid of this, it sounds techy, but it is as simple as choosing the .csv option when saving the file. The email addresses you upload are matched to registered users.

If you're using a real estate specific tool or software (ex. "Top Producer"), or any other CRM format, check the product's documentation to see whether contact export to one of the above formats is available.

## Vanity URL?

A URL is simply the address of a web page. For example, to get to Facebook, you'd type www.facebook.com or www.fb.com into your browser.

When your new FFP is first created, the URL might look something like this:

- https://www.facebook.com/pages/Social-Media-for-Real-Estate/349484765207343?ref=hl

Clearly, this is not a very user friendly, communicable or memorable link. However, once you reach 25 page likes, you can ditch the cumbersome digits to create your own personalized vanity URL.

You may want to call in some favors from 25 of your closest friends and family to get this done, sooner than later. However, make sure you choose friends who are relevant to your FFP to avoid detrimental page likes (see below).

Send an email or private message that includes your initial page URL and ask for those first page likes.

Once you've done this, you can choose a new URL, subject to availability, that may look something like this:

- https://www.facebook.com/CoastalNetTech (my husband's IT firm)

Much cleaner, memorable and easy to articulate!

To claim your unique vanity URL go to the *"about* section" of your fan page and access the web address section.

**Promote your vanity URL everywhere!** – Send a personalized message to a carefully selected list of your core and relevant fans. Copy and paste your newly generated vanity URL to <u>everything</u> you can think of, including your personal:

- Website
- Email signature
- Business card
- Landing page

**Embed your URL**! - It is super easy to embed your URL as a clickable hyperlink in text and images. For example, if you added a *"Follow me on Facebook"* tagline to your email signature, website or any other live document via most any platform like Word or Outlook, simply highlight the appropriate text to select it, right click and choose the hyperlink option from the dropdown menu. From here, you'll be able to insert your custom URL and change up the visible text (if desired). Follow the same procedure to embed your custom URL in an image. Here's how. Insert your image of choice, click on it to select, then right click to access the hyperlink options. Simple!

Audience power building tips

**Working Online Communities** - This is an extremely powerful audience building tool. Let's say one of the areas you do a lot of business in (or want to) is Cherry Hill, NJ. Type *"Cherry Hill NJ"* into Facebook's search bar. You'll get a massive list of groups, pages, places, communities and individual users related to Cherry Hill.

For example, some of the results I generated include: *Cherry Hill Moms' Group, Cherry Hill Mall, and Cherry Hill Youth & Athletic Club.*

- You'll want to investigate all page and group results of interest to assure they're legitimate and active. Once you have:
    - Consider joining relevant pages and groups.
    - Post to these pages as your FFP (not your FP) for exposure.
    - Participate in the conversation.
    - Locate the page owners, administrators and any key contributors. Consider sending them personal invitations to your FFP.
    - Share relevant content from these pages back on your own FFP.

Quora - is a question-and-answer website where questions are created, answered, edited and organized by its community of users. After signing-up for your free account, search for real estate related topics and provide expert responses. Post new questions for the community and add links to your website, FFP or blog. Incredibly effective at building credibility!

Detrimental page likes

In simple terms, a detrimental page like means doing anything necessary to gain irrelevant fans. Typically, this is accomplished by:

- Asking any *"human"* you can find - requesting core fans to ask their friends and friends of friends to like your FFP, regardless of their relevance to your page. If these people are not in your target market, short of a possible relocation lead, they're not going to be interested in what you have to say and will likely unfollow, hide or even unlike your FFP. These are negative behaviors noted by Facebook that will penalize your FFP.

- Buying "Likes" - another way detrimental page likes are accumulated is by paying for likes via services that promise you a certain number of likes for a fee. Often, these page likes are not real people and/or are out of the country and therefore completely irrelevant.

39

- <u>Participating in *"like exchange groups"*</u> - when you join one of these groups you agree to like each other's FFPs. Here again, you're gathering potentially irrelevant fans.

**Beware detrimental page likes -** If you ever decide to use paid Facebook advertising, every detrimental page like you have will cost you money to reach fake accounts or irrelevant fans. In other words, having friends, family and colleagues that are not in your target market, will water-down your advertising efforts and ultimately cost you money.

Beneficial page likes

Beneficial page likes are likes from past, present and future clients, in addition to locals **likely** to use your services. We consider these fans relevant

However, the better you know your target audience, the more beneficial your page likes will be. In other words, do you prefer working with buyers or sellers, 1st time home buyers or rentals? What's the age demographic of your primary client base? Price range? Married, single, men, women, families, empty nesters, snow birds, investors? All of this should become very clear to you based on the previous **friend evaluation** process.

Define and focus on your niche. Resist worrying about losing a deal by possibly leaving someone out of targeted conversations. No one can be all things to all people. Here's an example, if your primary market consisted of primarily urban condo sales and first time homebuyers, yet you worry about appealing to the few investor clients in your *sphere of influence*, you probably won't have a very effective strategy.

I learned this the hard way early in my career. I'd established a strong niche with trade-up sellers in a specific geographic area. My boss at the time, a successful commercial broker, pushed me to duplicate his success with big ticket commercial sales. It didn't go well. I didn't have the knowledge, connections or interest to work this type of business. It failed miserably and took time away from my core business connections. You all know what type of customer you work well with. If you don't like or feel comfortable with a certain business niche, you won't do a good job and your self-esteem will take a hit. Be true to yourself.

**The core value of beneficial page likes -** When you accumulate truly beneficial fans, you are in a unique position to use Facebook's targeting algorithms to your advantage. Beneficial page likes, as discussed above, are comprised of relevant fans who've made the first step on the "path of interest." You can more easily target the things you say and do on your FFP more powerfully."

## Call-to-action

It is important to coax your fans to engage with you off-Facebook, to capture prospect information and maintain communication due to ever changing Facebook algorithms.

To do this, simply access your FFP's call to action tool. After set-up, your visitors will be directed to your choice of landing pages <u>outside</u> of Facebook.

## Tabs

This is an optional DIY you can easily install in minutes. Tabs are a great way to diversify and organize your FFPs content, while creating a polished and professional page look. To install tabs, simply type *"static Iframe tabs"* in the search Facebook field. You'll have some options here with instructions for installation and customization. It's super easy and upon completion, you can congratulate yourself on installing your very first Facebook app!

**More on Iframes -** Don't let the tech sound of this tool scare you off. Simply put, an Iframe is tech jargon for a window frame that holds outside content (or off-Facebook content), such as your personal or company website. Consider adding a "welcome page tab" or a "search listings tab," just to name a few. Tabs can link to a landing page, your personal website, opt-in page or sign-up page to collect the valuable off-Facebook prospect information mentioned above. Advanced "Tab" Options for consideration are your website's property search page or a direct link (if available) to your MLS's consumer facing web portal.

Again, these are suggestions only. As mentioned earlier, the success of your page does not hinge on how "high tech" your page is.

## Understanding Edge Rank

This is a meaty topic and not necessarily something you need to grasp as a beginner. Below are some highlights. However, in the quest to be thorough, additional details can be found in the *"Glossary of Terms"* section of this manual:

- An algorithm is a formula. Edge Rank is **one** of Facebook's formulas that generates what you see in your newsfeed and to some degree, sponsored ads.
- Edge Rank contains over 10,000 variables that predict our *relationships* with pages and friends. It discerns which content users see in their newsfeeds.
- Edge Rank criteria is constantly changing. You may have noticed the disappearance of previously prominent posts from friends and pages.

## Newsfeed worthy?

Now that we know there's an algorithm (formula) that decides which content makes it to our newsfeeds, it's helpful to understand Edge Rank's prioritization:

- Photos/native video – Facebook's native video is treated with priority (an attempt to overthrow YouTube).
- Links – source quality here is **king.** A website or blog with many social media interactions and credibility is prioritized.
- Text posts – the greatest range but potentially the lowest engagement.

## Posting strategies

Using the information you collected earlier to create a core list of topics and interests, sort them from high to low, based on the number of fans that align with each topic. This provides a prioritized content list that you can rotate or "weight" towards the most in-demand topics, if desired.

## Optimal posting times

It's not surprising that the less people want to work at their jobs, the more they login to Facebook! Appropriate posting times impact how often posts are seen and engaged with. Here's what we know:

- Thursday-Friday, early afternoon
- 1pm – gets most shares
- 3pm – gets most clicks
- There's a "*happiness index*" that spikes by 10% on Fridays. ("Happiness index" analyzes the use of positive and negative words in status updates to estimate the happiness of people on Facebook.)
- 86% of posts are published during the work week

## Organic reach

Users who see your posts in their timeline, when you post them (without paid or boosted posts).

## Paid reach

Paid reach is exactly as it sounds. Paid ads or boosts (by you) to assure visibility. The amount of money spent per paid reach depends on the post and post content.

## Viral reach

Multi-level sharing of any of your original posts to friends, friends of friends and beyond.

Viral reach will include users who are not your followers, but they see your posts because their friends shared it with them.

### Timeliness decay

Older posts are typically hidden from newsfeeds. Only new and recent posts will appear. Post 5-7 times per week to ensure timeliness is not decayed and posts are visible to your fans.

### Diverse content

Post diverse content, including text, images, videos and links to everything that adds weight and engages the attention of your audience.

Active engagement of your fans boosts the visual frequency of your posts. Since timeliness is one of the most basic components of Edge Rank, post with a frequency that your audience will not miss. Avoid sharing old posts and links that will automatically set user preferences to lower levels and preclude the visibility of your posts.

### Spamming

Remember, an excess of anything is bad. Avoid posting so frequently that you earn the infamous spammer label!

### Content composition

The basic rule:

- <u>20% real estate content</u> **MAXIMUM -** Your new listings, open houses, price reductions. More preferably information, advice, problems and solutions.)
- <u>80% diverse and engaging content</u> - Based on the evaluation of your existing and future fans

### Fan engagement

The engagement of your fans is the most important component of your page's success.

Non-monetary contests, surveys, quizzes and fill-in-the-blank activities are excellent engagement tools.  For example:

- Caption contest - provide a sketch or visual of some kind and ask for a caption.
- Questions – for example, "which US state has the highest single family sales price?"
- Where would you live – "If you could live anywhere, where would it be?" Potential answers: waterfront, rural, subdivision, urban, etc.
- Seasonal – "what kind of house would …. (Santa, Cupid, Uncle Sam) live in?"
- Motivational and inspirational quotes.
- Clean humor and photos (G rated)
- Water-cooler talk:
  - "Did you catch the Phillies' game last night?"
  - "Which team will win the Super Bowl?"

**Your 1st Fan -** don't forget to like your own page once created, and be sure to congratulate yourself for doing it!

Social capital

The premise of social capital stems from the realization that our social networks have value. The people within these networks do things for each other, such as buying products, sharing articles, and helping each other. Relationships are currency. When cashed in, it's what you can ask people to do that ultimately benefits you personally.

A new agent I once worked with had absolutely no real estate or prior sales experience. However, she'd been an administrative assistant for a local church with an extremely large congregation for several years. She'd fostered tremendous goodwill in that role. Working these connections, launched an impressive career in lightning speed. In this example, finding clients was not obstacle. Gaining the expertise to serve them well was. By teaming with a seasoned agent for a time, expertise and demand for service were met.

The hitch to social capital is that you can only take out what you put in, much like a bank account. If you're always asking for business, instead of contributing, your balance will run negative quickly.

Make social capital deposits often, and build up your balance well before you ask your audience to buy what you're selling. Do this by being helpful and creating value for as many people in your audience as possible. At its core, social capital depends on what you can provide for your audience that builds trust, value and credibility. Simply put, providing readily available relevant content and timely advice on your FFP will accomplish this.

**Tips on building social capital** - make genuine personal connections with your audience. Show concern by offering assistance. Engage people in conversation that you enjoy talking with, even if there's no financial gain:

- Keep in touch with others that you've helped, or who have helped you. Send personal emails to see what's new, or how a personal problem worked out.
- Be of assistance, whenever possible, in small ways.
- Volunteer!
- Answer questions on message boards and give advice when asked.
- Give value to your audience, for free. Share real estate market trends and statistics.
- Put together a DIY guide of some sort.
- Segue into podcasts, blog posts and webinars.
- Think out of the box to show your gratitude. Consider video/audio thanks, handwritten notes, social media praise.
- Referrals beget referrals! Do you have an awesome chiropractor, handyman or dentist? Praise and endorse their services. Odds are, you'll create a mutually beneficial advocacy.
- Seek out local small business groups to form alliances with on and offline. These groups typically allow membership to **one** member from each business specialty. Members are encouraged to use each other's services regularly.
- Know of a local freebie, great deal or coupon? Shout it out to your fans! An example, Rita's Ice gives away free ices on the 1st day of spring each year. Remind your fans to stop by and grab theirs!

- Support community fund raisers. Perhaps your high school swim team is offering $5 car washes to raise money, or the local Knights of Columbus is doing a bake sale. Get behind these events, get known and enjoy the reciprocity.

## Know your audience

This section will make you laugh as you relate your current friends and fans to the personas below. Knowing the various personality types of your audience is a positive step in the cultivation of social marketing.

Disclaimer: Understanding personality types **does not** mean we fuel the fire of the few *"negative nellies"* or *"conspiracy theorists"* amongst our friends and fans. Your goal is to remain neutral and stay away from anything negative or judgmental. Always think Switzerland!

As you may have noticed, Facebook is a terrific profiling tool. If you want to know someone, follow their posts for a time. Knowing the type of person you're dealing with will give you a "leg up" when you need to interact with them on a professional level.

You'll find numerous and varying descriptions of Facebook user types throughout the web, all of which are generalizations subject to interpretation. The following are my unique and admittedly unscientific profiles:

- The "Average User" – 100-200 friends. Logs in once or twice a day, scans over posts, comments occasionally, clicks "like" only if they actually like the comment, picture, etc. Morbid curiosity alone drives their daily check-ins.
- The "Addict" – the compulsive user who never logs-out. Has the app on his phone running side-by-side with his laptop. More prevalent in younger users. The motivator for this user is fear of missing something.
- The "Lurker" – never posts or comments, yet reads and internalizes everything on their newsfeed. You may run into this person in the supermarket and be shocked to hear well wishes regarding your recent flu.

- The "Laugher" – says nothing aside from LOL and LMAO's to anything and everything. This user has communication difficulties, is shy or frightened by technology.
- The "Hoarder" – has thousands of friends just to appear popular. Will friend anyone to crank his or her friend count. Studies reveal these folks are inherently insecure.
- The "Egotist" – Look at my life, my children, my house, my exotic vacations and cars. An obvious need for envy and superiority.
- The "Gamer" – plays games day long. This is probably the extent of their engagement.
- The "Holy Roller"– everything they post references personal religious beliefs along with various, sometimes lengthy proselytization of "my way is the only way."
- The "Miserable" – hates their life, whines about the color of the sky and any other trivialities they can come up with. This group would manage to find a problem with anything!
- The "Critter Lover" – be it cats, dogs, ferrets, etc. you'll see way too many daily pics of critter broods, along with an assortment of internet animal memes.
- The "Over-Exposer" – sharing meal photos, hour-by-hour updates on where they've been, where they're going and who they're with. Overall, a detailed account of absolute minutia driven by a quest for friends.
- The "Belonger" – never posts, yet joins every group to feel part of something simply to claim he is.
- "Liker" – never comments, just clicks the like button straight down her newsfeed. This user doesn't have much to say, but feels obliged to affirm everyone's posts to save face.
- The "Politician" – prone to frequent rants of disdain for any political figure not on their side of the aisle. Typically, this user is an all or nothing thinker whose identity is tightly aligned to his stance. Nothing you say or do will prod them from their position. Compromise and middle ground are not options.
- The "Causer" – non-stop posting about their cause, as if no one else had one and as if it were the only cause worthy enough to acknowledge. This user uses their cause to keep their true selves at bay. Send periodic support.

- The "Critic" – this user loves to point out what's wrong with society, today's youth, the world and even the cable company! Posts often start with "when I was a kid …. *(Blah, blah, blah -- insert topic here)."* Aside from this users' proclivity for negativity, dissatisfaction with personal achievements is at the core of their behavior.
- The "Duped" – these users urgently warn of "Bill Gates' plan to charge everyone $1 per sent and received email. Pass this post on to show your protest! Most often this user is harmless, just a tad ignorant.
- The "Chainer" – pass this poem along to 10 of your friends within the next 20 minutes or the ceiling will fall on your head. This user is inherently superstitious and truly believes they'll be cursed if requests are not honored within the prescribed time frame.

## Prep Work

Spend 1-2 weeks stocking your FFP with content, prior to official page invitations. Make sure your FFP is visually appealing, contains a welcome page and/or the activated call to action option for lead capture and opt-ins.

## Marketing plan

Complete the following activities **5x each**, every 30 days:

- Post a comment as your FFP to your FP.
- Post a comment as your FP to your FFP (the reverse of the above).
- Share a post from related community pages you've discovered.
- Chat – say "hello" in real time. Nothing fancy, a simple "hey, how are you?"
- Like a friend or fans' status.
- Comment on a friend or fans' post.
- Update your status, say what's going on in your world (in a professional manner, of course).
- Tag yourself and/or others in relevant politically correct photos.
- Post a relevant photo or video.
- Post an inspirational or motivational quote.

- Post relevant places (check-ins) - for security purposes, post these once you leave the destination. (ex., attended the *"Triple Play Real Estate Convention and Expo"*).
- Endorse a local business or service you love.
- Share coupons and deals
- Acknowledge/support a community event or cause.
- Share an area specific statistic or news article
- Post with a topical (#) hashtag.

As available:

- Post a buyer/seller testimonial.
- Welcome a new homeowner (recent buyer closings) to the neighborhood.
- Thank a recent seller for using your services.

## Hashtags

Hashtags are a word or phrase preceded by a hash or pound sign (#), and are used to identify messages on a specific topic. By including topical hashtags, your posts have the ability to propel your content beyond your FP and/or FFP's audience.

Hashtag trends change by the minute. Make it a habit to take a look at trending hashtags from time to time and see if there's anything relevant to your niche that you can share or add to the conversation mix. To find trending hashtags, check out hashtags.org (or #hashtags.org). This site uses Twitter's streaming API (a techy application index) to identify prominent posts and users. An example: Let's say you are an agent in Houston, TX and Beyoncé, a native Houstonian, is up for a *"Grammy."* A relevant post might be:

*"Good Luck at the #Grammys Tonight #Beyoncé, from all your Hometown Fans in #HoustonTX".*

**Prominent real estate hashtags** - Below are some widely used real estate hashtags to consider using regularly to blast your content:

- #RealEstate
- #Realtor
- #Realty
- #Broker
- #ForSale
- #NewHome
- #HouseHunting
- #MillionDollarListing
- #HomeSale
- #HomesForSale
- #Property
- #Properties
- #Investment
- #Home
- #Housing
- #Listing
- #Mortgage
- #HomeInspection
- #CreditReport
- #CreditScore
- #Foreclosure
- #NAR
- #EmptyNest
- #Renovated
- #JustListed

**Create your own unique hashtags:**

- #YourName - (ex.  #JohnJones, or #realestatebyjohnjones)
- #YourOfficeName - (ex. #AnytownRealtypropertiesforsale)

**Event hashtags:**

- #OpenHouse - (ex. #bobsopenhouse, #123mainstreetopenhouse)

**Geographic hashtags ideas:**

- #HomesforSalePhiladelphia
- #Philadelphia
- #CondosforSaleLasVegas
- #LasVegas

Get creative and have fun using hashtags!

## Define your initial value offer

As your page grows, carefully consider the value you provide to a visiting user who'll hopefully do business with you.

- Do you provide DIY tips?
- An e-book for *"1ˢᵗ time homebuyers?"*
- *"101 Things to see"* in specific areas?
- *"Most important things to know"* about real estate in Anytown, USA?

## Content curation

The concern I hear most often from agents in the field is "where do I get content?" In reality, it is impossible to be short on content. Limitless free content is available to you with the click of a mouse. Here are just a few of the numerous resources available to you:

1. Personal or company websites and agent portals– share real estate information and articles about you and your company from your company website and agent portal. Does your company website have interactive consumer tools (ex., mortgage calculator, affordability calculator)?

2. Visual market statistics – graphs on trends from your local MLS – average list and sales prices, absorption rates, days on market comparisons, etc.
3. Real estate specific news - stories from industry outlets like Inman and RISMedia.
4. Your loan officer – mortgage rates, new programs and incentives. Information on specialty programs like 1st time homebuyer and jumbo loan programs.
5. Local chamber of commerce – local events and community information.
6. School district information – school ratings, programs, sports, upcoming events, fund raisers.
7. Town or area community pages –area events, gatherings, causes, issues.
8. National, state and local REALTOR® Association websites – real estate news, videos blogs, homeownership research, statistics and trends.
9. Google alerts – set-up several keyword alerts to generate news and community stories related to the towns, counties and areas you serve (ex., Tucson Real Estate, Condos, NAR, etc).
10. ISPs (internet service providers) - sites like Yahoo, Hotmail and MSN, to name a few, have endless quantities of well-rounded content available for immediate sharing, including business, trending news, videos, local and world news and lifestyle articles.
11. Content aggregators: aggregators are websites or programs that collect related content and display them or link to them. These are just a few examples:
    a. StumbleUpon.com – this is one of my favorite tools. Based on the information you obtained by vetting your friends' interests, add topics of interest to this site and you'll be randomly directed to truly unique, conversation worthy, often obscure web content. Similar options include:
        i. Umano.com (an audio news magazine)
        ii. Flipboard.com (topical news magazine)
        iii. RSS Feeds - or *"really simple syndication,"* is a feed used to publish frequently updated information from blog entries, news headlines, audio and video. Don't let the name scare you. Compile a list of sites or blogs you regularly follow (or want to), along

with topics of interest on behalf of your fans. You'll receive a daily feed that includes full or summarized text and articles ready to share. RSS feeds can be set up through many of your email clients (ex., Outlook), but I've found it easier to utilize a tool called *feedly.com*. There's literally no set-up involved, same great timely content and it suggests new topics based on your interests.

12. <u>Public Domain</u> – public domain refers to un-copyrighted materials. You are free to use this information without cost or permission. Perform a public domain search on specific topics of interest. You'll be amazed at what you come up with. Tons of free content, images, text and more. Public domain content can help you put together free e-books for your fans quickly and legally.

13. <u>Private Label Rights (PLR)</u> – PLR articles are a relatively new twist on content building. Private label rights are a special type of right or license available for purchase, which allows you to legally edit and publish articles as your own. You may even include your own name as the author and your own resource box at the end of each article. PLR articles are a relatively inexpensive way to produce content. Search "private label rights" and you'll find a host of content pre-packaged for immediate use for little or no cost.

14. <u>Usa.gov</u> - is an easy-to-search, free-access website designed to give you a centralized place to find information from U.S. local, state, and federal government agency websites.

15. <u>Ezinearticles.com</u> - an article directory that accepts unpaid submissions from authors, in exchange for links to the authors' websites and visibility for their work. The site also allows web and Ezine publishers to freely republish articles from the site, subject to certain conditions.

16. <u>Pikmonkey.com</u> – this free photo editor will take your photos from boring to awesome. Apply effects, filters and post!

17. <u>Stock Photos, Illustrations, Images</u> - royalty free, or low fee stock photos, vector art illustrations, stock footage and audio for print. Here are just a few of the numerous resources available on the web:
    a. *Istockphoto.com*
    b. *Freedigitalphotos.net*
    c. *Creativecommons.org*
    d. *Morguefile.com*

18. Infographics – increasingly popular! A well-designed infographic can help you simplify a complicated subject, or turn an otherwise boring subject into a captivating experience. Get your creative side going and create a custom masterpiece, or search *Pinterest.com* (another great general resource for visuals), for infographics specific to real estate or other topics of interest to your fans. (Remember to credit source authors when you share!) Create your own infographic with any of these resources:
    a. *Piktochart.com*
    b. *Infogr.am*
    c. *Visual.ly*
    d. *Venngage.com*
19. Canva.com – An absolute personal favorite of mine. Canva gives you everything you need to easily turn ideas into stunning designs. Create custom designs for Facebook covers and posts, and so much more.
20. mine.relsci.com - MINE delivers the most relevant news and finely curated articles on the people and businesses that matter most to you. MINE provides an escape from the deluge of blog posts, tweets, status updates, work anniversaries and endorsements. Instead, it delivers actionable business intelligence for your professional network.
21. portent.com – headline generator. Type in your topic and click for multiple headline options. Be careful, this leans towards the dramatic!
22. woobox.com - helps you easily create powerful contests, sweepstakes, coupons, and more to grow your fans and amplify marketing.
23. BuzzSumo.com - a great place to see which topics, related to your business, get the most attention, and ability to do more of what works. You can get detailed insights about what type of content people are sharing, how that content is formatted and how you can make it better to get even more shares than the last person.
24. coschedule.com/headline-analyze - free headline analyzer and writer of awesome headlines for blog posts and email subject lines that drive social shares, traffic, and SEO value.

1. wishpond.com - create landing pages, contests, promotions, forms, popups, ads & email campaigns using Wishpond.
2. audacity.com – free audio recording software for podcast creation, amongst other things.
3. 3d-pack.com – one of many 3d-box graphic generators. 3d package lets you instantly create 3d-box images online, free! Just upload pictures for cover and sides and then get 3d-box in your favorite image format (JPG, GIF, PNG) and post them anywhere.
4. podomatic.com – a website specialized in the creation of tools and services that enable users to easily find, create, distribute, promote and listen to both audio and video podcasts.
5. leadpages.com – an easy landing page generator. Build conversion optimized & mobile responsive landing pages.
6. optimizepress.com – another landing/sales page generator.
7. Fiverr.com - an online marketplace offering tasks and services (graphic design, SEO, content and so much more), beginning at a cost of $5 per job performed. The site is primarily used by freelancers to offer a variety of different services, and by customers to buy those services. Some similar options:
    a. Elance.com
    b. Odesk.com
8. Yoast.com – SEO optimization. Optimize your posts to get ranked within Google and generate traffic.
9. Bufferapp.com - Buffer makes scheduling all of your posts easy. Spend an hour setting up posts and have your entire social media schedule set-up for a week. It's really simple to use and has a great free plan to help you get started.
10. Trello.com - get organized. Trello is a simple, free tool that helps you organize your thoughts in a format somewhat similar to a Pinterest board. It will replace any to-do list you currently use after you try it.
11. ZenPen.com - is a free tool that lets you write in an elegant format and stay focused. You can see your content start to take shape in a beautiful and minimalist format. Write in ZenPen, then copy and paste into your desired format. An uncomplicated alternative to Word.

## Word blocking

Consider setting up some word blocks to avoid negative fan posts. This could be competitor names or any individual or combination of words or phrases like "bad service, unprofessional, etc." that you wouldn't want showing up on your page. When fans include a word you've blocked, the post will automatically be marked as spam. Access settings and page moderation to add blocked words. To unmark a post or comment as spam, go to the spam section of your FFP's activity log.

## Profanity filter

You can block various degrees of profanity from appearing on your page. Facebook determines what to block by using the most commonly reported words and phrases marked offensive by the community. Select your preferred filter strength (medium or strong) from the profanity filter section of settings.

## Dwindling organic reach

In our overview of Edge Rank, one of Facebook's algorithms, we reviewed why constant changes and restrictions can negatively impact your page's organic reach. You may have noticed this yourself as various, once prominent pages and posts disappeared from your personal newsfeed. We call this dwindling organic reach.

Dwindling organic reach is one reason we look to capture contact information and/or opt-ins to our newsletter, blog.

## Pay to play

The reality is Facebook won't change its reach restrictions in the near future. Once your page is up and functional, consider setting aside whatever nominal marketing dollars you can afford to extend your reach.

Studies show successive mini-boosts of posts for a mere $5-$10 each, have positive lingering effects on your page's overall reach. Set a budget to boost a few <u>meaningful</u> posts

<u>Types of paid advertising</u> - First, determine what you want to accomplish:

- More likes?
- Post promotion?

## Paid advertising tips

- Target your market – at least 50,000 recommended. Be as local specific as you can with zip codes. It costs more but less is wasted.
- Don't run campaigns continuously. Kill ads late night/early morning.
- Create separate campaigns based on fan interests and 3 year demographic age brackets to quickly identify what's working and what's not.
- "Click if you agree" strategies work well.
- Be specific. While it sounds overly simplistic, users need you to tell them exactly what to do. Ex. "Click here to sign-up for a free real estate investors' guide."
- Pay based on cpc (cost per click) not cpm (cost per thousand-impressions).
- Videos and photos work best. Blog posts, not as much.
- Budget $5-10 per post is enough.

## Advanced custom apps

We've discussed adding tabs and Iframes to your FFP fairly early on for the purpose of opt-in and lead capture. Once you have a decent fan base, consider adding apps that link to platforms like your Pinterest, YouTube and Twitter presences. Apps are easier to install than you think. For example, if you wanted to find a Pinterest app to add to your page, simply type *"Pinterest app"* in the Facebook search field, as you did with the iframe search.

## Facebook marketing on auto-pilot

To create a post that's scheduled to appear on your page at a specific date and time, go to *"power editor"* at www.facebook.com/ads/manage/powereditor.

As you grow, consider hiring a Facebook page manager and/or content curator who can assist with schedules, content, reply and respond to comments, run engagement reports (what worked, what didn't), handle complaints and spammers. Recent college grads are great for this, but must be socially savvy.

## Editorial calendar

Your FFP is your own social publishing platform. Think of this as real estate owned. I recommend creating a schedule 3 months in advance. This will help you visualize your plan and keep you on schedule.

## Don't abandon ship

Frustration is understandable in the beginning. However, think twice before abandoning your efforts.

With over 1 billion active Facebook users each month, it is impossible to make the necessary quality personal touches through any other social media platform.

If you become overwhelmed, dial it back a bit. Grab your editorial calendar for the upcoming month and cut your planned activities in half to give yourself a breather. Continue to scale back and rev back up, as needed. Lean on the post scheduler tool to set-up activities in one sitting.

Thanks for reading. Wishing you all the very best of luck in all your endeavors!

# Glossary of Terms

Below are a few common terms. Please visit Facebook's Help Section at www.Facebook.com/Help for a complete up to date resource.

## Activity Log

Your page's activity log helps you manage your timeline. Review your posts and comments by your page.

## Application (app)

The short answer, a program that allows users to share content and interact with others and enhance your experience on Facebook. Often thought of as games. However, custom apps are available for business pages as well, which can link to an organization's website or landing page and much more.

## Audience Selector

You'll find an audience selector tool most places you share status updates, photos and other things you post. Click the tool and select the specific audience you want to share something with. Options include public, friends, family and any custom lists and groups you've created, as well as private messages.

## Blocking

If someone's bothering you on Facebook, blocking is the best way to stop them. If you were friends, the step would automatically unfriend reciprocally.

## Call to Action

Available on FFPs only. Select one of seven buttons, which use verbs to attempt to get user conversion and appear on top of the cover photo.

The options are:

- Book Now
- Contact Us
- Use App
- Play Game

- Shop Now
- Sign Up
- Watch Video

## Check-In

Users who wish to announce their location to their friends on Facebook can tap a check-in button to see a list of places nearby via their mobile device's GPS system. Your check-in will create a story in your friends' newsfeeds and show up in the recent activity section on the page for that place.

## Comment

Responding to something that is already on Facebook. (Ex. Your friend posts about the movie they saw this weekend. You respond with a comment of some sort --"Yes, hoping to see that movie as well."

## Edge Rank

An algorithm is used to determine what content gets shown on individual users' newsfeeds. An algorithm is basically a formula. In Facebook's case, an ever changing formul. Facebook's primary algorithm is Edge Rank.

## Edge Rank components:

- Affinity – this index relates to the frequency we've shared or hidden posts from a liked page. You may have noticed that pages you've liked don't always show up in your newsfeed. Facebook decided that you want to identify with a specific page (because you're a fan) but you don't want to interact with it. In a situation like this, the page disappears from your newsfeed and is replaced with the one whose posts you like. To resume newsfeed posts from a specific page, go to the page's timeline and like some posts.

- Weight – Facebook posts have various weights. For example, photos have higher weights than text posts. A post that gets hundreds of likes in a short time will gain more visibility. The post that gets hundreds of likes in five minutes will gain more visibility than the post with only 10 likes.

In addition, weight looks at whether a post was shared by someone with a wide network of friends/followers, and whether said post was largely hidden by users (with the assumption that they didn't like it).

- Time Decay – this component of Edge Rank describes when our last interaction with the page took place. If we've interacted with a page or a friend quite recently, it is likely that a future post will be displayed in our newsfeed. The more popular or heavier a post is, the odds improve for breaking through the plethora of other posts, despite past interactivity.

- Last Actor – this variable is related to our last 50 actions on Facebook. It matches a part of posts even if, according to Edge Rank, they shouldn't be displayed. Let's say that 15 of those actions were comments on the page of a friend that we don't have a very strong relationship with. If it was so, future posts from this page would be shown.

- Story Bumping – consider a post that resulted in massive interaction. This particular post wasn't displayed on your wall, or perhaps you weren't active back then. Despite this, Facebook decided that this is an interesting piece of information from the user with whom you have high Affinity. In addition, this post is "heavy," because it was shared a lot. Assume this particular post is about something you're not interested in. Maybe you saw it once, and skipped it. You'll notice in cases like this that Facebook pushes the post to the top of your feed simply because another friend wrote and commented on it and/or it has many likes. Unfortunately, hiding the post will result in minus Affinity points. What might happen next is that the person that posted it will disappear from your newsfeed.

Fan
A fan is someone who chooses to like an organization's business or fan page, not a personal page.

### Fan Page, Like Page, Business Page

All the same thing, although depending on the type of business, the categories will be different. This is the business side of Facebook. People connect by clicking the like button. Unlimited number of likes are allowed.

### Friend

A personal connection via your Facebook personal presence or FP, not your business page or FFP. A fan is someone who likes your fan page by clicking like.

### Groups

Groups are dedicated spaces where you can share updates, photos or documents and message other group members. You can also select one of three privacy options for each group you create. Privacy settings can be set by the group creator to public, closed or secret. (*ex., "Anytown Realty Agents Group"*).

### Hashtags

Hashtags turn topics and phrases into clickable links in your posts on your FP or FPP. This helps people find posts about topics they're interested in. To make a hashtag, write # (the number sign) along with a topic or phrase and add it to your post. For example, *#IloveRealEstate*.

When you click a hashtag, you'll see a feed of posts that include that hashtag. You may also see some related hashtags at the top of the page. A hashtag must be one word (no spaces). You can search for a hashtag using the search bar at the top of any page.

### Life Events

Specific to FPs only. The life event option lets you add experiences from the different parts of your life to your timeline. Life events are divided into categories (ex: work & education, family & relationships), and you can use them to share many different kinds of important moments, from an engagement, vacation or a new baby or home. Unlike other stories, life events will automatically be starred on your timeline. Beware, they are also public by default, but you can adjust the audience at any time using the audience selector.

## Likes

There are different types of likes:

- When you click the like button on a business or fan page, you are now a fan of that page.
- Liking individual posts and comments of others.
- On your own business/ban page - # of likes are the total # of users that like your page.

## Lists

Available on FPs only. Organized groupings of friends that you create.

## Milestones

Available on FPs only. Milestones are a special type of page post that let you highlight key moments on your page's timeline. You can use milestones to share important events that tell the story of what your page is about. For details, see Facebook Help.

## Newsfeed

An aggregation or compilation of friends' posts and comments and pages you like and follow. An ever changing algorithm or formula, as created and applied by Facebook, is constantly tweaked, thus changing the content of your newsfeed often. See algorithm above.

## Page

Often used to describe both FPs and FFPs, Pages are actually the official public presence for businesses, organizations, artists, public figures, professionals, causes or products.

## Page Administrators

Persons who create and manage activity in groups or pages. There are 5 different types of roles for people who manage pages. Only an administrator can change someone's role. For details, see page roles at Facebook Help.

## Page Insights

Available for FFPs only. Insights provide information about your FFP's performance and are available after at least 30 people like your FFP. Find demographic data about your audience, and see how people are discovering and responding to your posts.

## Page Names

Name your page(s) carefully. Avoid improper capitalization and terms or phrases that may be abusive or violate someone's rights. Page names must use grammatically correct capitalization and may not include all capital letters (except for acronyms), symbols (ex: ®), unnecessary punctuation or any variation of the word "Facebook." Learn more at Facebook Brand Resources. Avoid misleading words. If a page isn't the official page of a brand, place, organization or public figure, the page name can't mislead others into thinking it's an official page or that it's managed by an authorized representative. Page names can't consist only of generic words (ex: Hamburgers). Pages must be managed by official representatives of the topics they're about.

## Page Post Metrics

Available for FFPs only. In the posts section of your Page Insights, you can see the following information about your page posts:

- The number of people your post reached.
- The number of people who clicked your post.
- The number of people who liked, commented on or shared your post.

If you post a video, you can also see the total number of video views and more details about viewing behavior.

## Personal Profile

Personal presence. Your personal page is a compilation of individual users for sharing and interaction.

### Places

Add a destination (ex. The Eiffel Tower, Paris France), or a business (i.e. Jim's Ice Cream Palace). Some businesses will give you discounts and/or coupons for checking-in at their location, or posting a favorable comment about their business or service.

### Posting

Essentially making a comment, sharing a photo, video or article. Posts can be date and time stamped, include friend tags (see below), add a location or check-in. Posts can be sent within groups and/or to specific lists you create or made public.

### Power Editor and Ad Creation

Power Editor is a managing tool for creating bulk ads. If you don't need to create hundreds of ads at scale, we recommend using ad creation.

### Private Message

A private message can be sent to friends or any Facebook user that does not have the feature blocked to the public (non-friends). A private message is best described as a private in-box message, like an email, that shows up in the user's message/chat inbox. Private messages are only visible to the specified recipient(s). When a new message or chat is received, the user will see a notification.

### Publishing Rights

If you started a page called "Everything About Madonna," this would be considered misleading since you yourself are not Madonna, nor have the rights, as an official representative of Madonna. You'd probably lose your publishing rights. If you name your page "Jane Johnson's Salute to Madonna," there would be no assumption of official affiliation.

### Status Update

A written post letting your friends know what you're thinking or doing.

### Tabs

A Facebook tab is a separate page (commonly referred to as a "tab") that can display a variety of categorized things within your FFP. Businesses tend to use custom Facebook tabs to welcome new visitors, offer discounts or coupons, showcase videos or other content, and more.

### Tag Review

Tag review is an option that lets you approve or dismiss tags that people add to your posts. Once activated, any time someone you in a post, that tag won't appear until you approve it. A recommended means to moderate content.

### Tagging

When you tag someone, you create a link to their profile. The post you tag the person in may also be added to that person's timeline. For example, you can tag a photo to show who's in the photo, or post a status update and say who you're with. If you tag a friend in your status update, anyone who sees that update can click on your friend's name and go to their profile. Your status update may also show up on that friend's timeline. When you tag someone, they'll be notified. Also, if you or a friend tags someone in your post, the post could be visible to the audience you selected, plus friends of the tagged person. Tags in photos and posts from people you aren't friends with may appear in *timeline review* where you can decide if you want to allow them on your timeline. You can also choose to review tags by anyone, including your friends.

### URL

A URL is the web address of pages online. For example, www.Facebook.com.

### Use Facebook As

Ability to post as yourself (FP) vs. posting as your business presence (FFP).

### User Names

When you create your FP and any subsequent FFPs and community pages, you'll get a rather nasty looking URL that might look something like www.facebook.com/ghansche1234578%%l89. Not very user friendly. This URL is simply the address to your FP. Since you'll want to share both your FP and FFP addresses, you'll want to adjust these URLs as follows:

FP User Name – Go to your FP. Click settings and scroll to user name to choose an easier, more memorable name. Something that is easy to remember, but contains your name. When you type your desired user name into the user name field, Facebook will tell you whether the name is available or not. I changed my FP URL to www.facebook.com/ghansche. Much simpler than the original.

## Vanity URL

Similar to user names for FPs and profiles, a vanity name can be claimed once your FFP has 25 or more fans. To claim your unique vanity name (URL) go to your FFP, click the about tab, scroll down to Facebook web address and type in your desired name. For example, my husband's business page for his company, Coastal Network Technologies, was originally something like -- www.facebook.com/coastall96?89[[lp7985 but once we hit 25 fans, we were able to adjust this to www.facebook.com/CoastalNetTech. Much better!

## Wall

The primary space within a page (business or personal) for incoming and outgoing posts and status updates. FFPs and FPs both have independent walls.

##

www.ingramcontent.com/pod-product-compliance
Lightning Source LLC
Chambersburg PA
CBHW070847180526
45168CB00002B/984